Julius Zupitza

Zur Literaturgeschichte des Guy von Warwick

Julius Zupitza

Zur Literaturgeschichte des Guy von Warwick

ISBN/EAN: 9783743670587

Hergestellt in Europa, USA, Kanada, Australien, Japan

Cover: Foto ©Thomas Meinert / pixelio.de

Weitere Bücher finden Sie auf **www.hansebooks.com**

ZUR

LITERATURGESCHICHTE

DES

GUY VON WARWICK.

————

VON

JULIUS ZUPITZA.

WIEN, 1873.

IN COMMISSION BEI KARL GEROLD'S SOHN

BUCHHÄNDLER DER KAIS. AKADEMIE DER WISSENSCHAFTEN.

Aus dem Julihefte des Jahrganges 1873 der Sitzungsberichte der phil.-hist. Classe der kais. Akademie der Wissenschaften (LXXIV. Bd., S. 623) besonders abgedruckt.

Druck von Adolf Holzhausen in Wien
k. k. Universitäts-Buchdruckerei.

Es ist meine Absicht, mit der Zeit die sämmtlichen mittelenglischen Bearbeitungen der ursprünglich altfranzösisch abgefassten Erzählung von Guy von Warwick, am liebsten mit dem Original dazu, herauszugeben. Die gegenwärtige Arbeit, die den Hauptzweck hat, mich von einigem ·nebensächlichen Material zu befreien, benutze ich zugleich zu der inständigen Bitte an alle Fachgenossen diesseits und jenseits des Kanals, mir zur Ergänzung der mir bekannten oder unbekannten Lücken in meinen Sammlungen freundlichst behilflich sein zu wollen.

1. Ein Fragment und seine Stellung innerhalb der me. Bearbeitungen des altfranzösischen Guy von Warwick.

Das Sloane MS. Nr. 1044 im britischen Museum zu London enthält ‚Specimens of Ancient Hand Writings‘: unter diesen befindet sich (Fol. 345, Nr. 625) ein bisher ganz unbeachtet gebliebenes Fragment eines me. Guy von Warwick, das ich hier veröffentlichen und im weiteren Verlaufe dieses Aufsatzes durch S bezeichnen will. Der Katalog setzt es ins 15. Jahrhundert, aber ich glaube, dass Schrift und Sprache gestatten, es noch dem 14. zuzuweisen. Es ist ein einziges Pergamentblatt in klein Folio auf beiden Seiten in je zwei Spalten zu je 54 Zeilen beschrieben, so dass überhaupt 216 Verse erhalten sind. In der ersten Spalte der Vorderseite fehlen bis Vers 35 zum grössten Theil die Anfangsbuchstaben entweder vollständig

oder bis auf geringe Spuren: in dem ersterwähnten Falle sind
sie im Abdrucke eingeklammert, in dem anderen durch cursive
Schrift bezeichnet. In der ersten Zeile sind vor þonceþ allerdings noch Spuren von, wie es scheint, zwei Buchstaben er-
kennbar: da es sich indessen nicht bestimmen liess, von welchen,
so habe ich das ganze von mir ergänzte þei eingeklammert.
Von V. 135 an bezeichnet aber die Klammer Unleserlichkeit,
cursiver Druck Undeutlichkeit der Handschrift. Die Absätze
sind nach der Hs. gemacht: wo die Verse eingerückt sind,
steht in ihr das bekannte §-Zeichen. Die Abkürzungen sind
aufgelöst, u und v, i und j geschieden.

        (þei) *þonkeþ* *god*, þat al haþ wrouȝt,   rᵃ
        (þ)at hym þider to hem haþ brouȝt,
        *A*nd prayeþ ȝerne wiþ boþe her honde:
        ,*G*od, let hym never part of londe'.
  5 *S*ir Guy into a chambre gos,
        *H*ende Felice aȝeyn hym ros
        *A*nd wel sone to hir he skippeþ,
        *T*o gedre lovelych þei kisseþ.
        (þ)ei kisseþ and clippeþ ofte siþe:
 10 *N*e were þei never so glad ne bliþe.
        *O*n hir bed heo made him sitte,
        *T*iþinges of hym heo wold wete,
        *A*nd he hir telleþ alle his lif,
        *H*ow ofte he miȝt have take wif,
 15 *K*ynges douȝters and emperoures
        *W*iþ myche riches and grete honoures;
        *A*nd ȝet nolde he none take,
        *B*ote alle forsoke for hir sake.
        ,*M*y love', he seyde, ,wol nowhere lende
 20 (B)ut on þe, Felice, þat art so hende.
        *S*ey me þi wille, now ich am here;
        *F*or ich have bouȝt þi love ful dere'.
        ,*G*od þe forȝelde', heo seyde, ,sire Guy:
        *A*lso ich segge sikerly.
 25 *S*o help me þe king of hevene,
        *P*assed ben ȝeres sevene,
        (I)ch had be spoused sikerly,
        (ȝ)if þat ȝe nere, sire Guy,

(A)nd spared, sire, neizen or ten
30 Princes, dukes, riche men
Of many londes, of grete honoures,
þat me desireden paramoures.
My fader wold have be glad,
ʒif ich ever wolde eny have had,
35 And pult me ofte to resoun,
Bote ay ich fonde gode enchesoun
For to putte it in delay;
For ich ne schal nouʒt, by þis day,
To oþer man my love ʒive,
40 þan to þe, þe while ich lyve.
Sir Guy vaillaunt and curteis,
Ich ʒelde me to þe', heo seis.
,Ich am redy þi wille to wirche
þurʒ þe lawe of holy chirche'.
45 Sir Guy for joye cusseþ hir þrie
Wiþout more vileny:
þei telleþ and talkeþ boþe samen
And maken solace and grete gamen.
Whan þei hadde spoken, þat hem gode þinke,
50 Swete Felice þan axede drynke:
A mayde brouzt hir biforen
þe clare in þe bugle horn.
Felice to Guy drynkeþ þo:
Grete is þe love bitwene hem two.
55 Sir Guy, as hym bihoved nede,   rͪ
His leve he toke and hamward ʒede
And makeþ him glad niʒt and day:
Now al his care is went away.
Þe erl on a day after masse
60 Takeþ wiþ hym þe countasse:
In to a chambre þei beþ ygo
And cleped Felice to hem two.
To hir þei seyde in privete:
,We ne haveþ non oþer child but þe,
65 Wel þou wost, mayde ne knave:
Oure heritage þe falleþ have
To governe, whan þat we be dede.

2

Leve douȝter, herkne my rede:
Dukes, erles, grete sires

70 Ech richer, þan oþer, þe desires:
þou take one, wel þou wost,
On whom þi hert stondeþ most.
þou let hym wedde þe to wyve:
Half oure lond we wolleþ þe ȝive.'

75 ,Sire', heo seide, ,nouȝt þe ne greve:
Ich wol take counseyl by ȝoure leve
And wiþ inne þis þridde day
Answere, ȝif ich kan or may.'
,Douȝter, de par dieus,' þei seyn:

80 þe erl and his contasse turneþ aȝeyn.
Whan þe þrid day was comen,
þe erl to his douȝter þe wey haþ nomen
And seiþ: ,ich holde þe ȝepe and wis:
Sey me, douȝter, þin avis.'

85 ,Sire', heo seyde, ,take nouȝt an ille,
þouȝ ich segge ȝow my wille.
Ich schal chese, so mote ich þrive,
Bifore alle men, þat beþ alyve
(And þat man, ich mest desire,

90 þou knowest him wel, leve sire),
Guy of Warwik, þe bachelere:
In alle þe worlde nys non his pere.
Certes, ȝif he me forsake,
Oþer ne schal ich never take.'

95 ,Wel hastow seyde, by seynt Symoun!
Douȝter, have þou my benesoun:
Miche þank ich þe kan,
þat þou desirest þat noble man.
þurȝ him þou schalt honoured be.

100 Me were lever, þan þis cite,
For why ich wist þe wille of Guy;
And ich þe telle resoun, why:
Maydenes haveþ loved him paramours,
Kynges douȝtres and emperoures,

105 Better, riccher and fairer of ble,
þan ever were þou or ever schalt be.

Witnesse on þe maide Blaunchfloure,
Reigneres douȝter, þe emperoure
(In a turnay he hir wanne,   vᵃ
110 þat sauȝ for soþe many a man),
And also swete Florentyn,
þat for hym suffred myche pyn.
Nis man bitwene þis and Rome,
þat me were lever, þat þou nome.
115 Ich schal ful prively and ful stille
Undergo his purpos and his wille.'
Þe erl Rohaut on a day
Biddeþ sadel his palfray
For to hunt in þe friþ,
120 And sire Guy wendeþ him wiþ.
þe knyȝtes nomen venesoun
Wiþ houndes ful grete foisoun.
Whan tyme was, hamward þei drawen:
þes bolde men syngen and plawen.
125 þe erl Rohaut, sire Guy also
Riden talkyng bitwene hem two.
þe erle Rohaut, as he wel can,
Aresoneþ Guy, þat noble man:
‚Sire Guy', he seide, ‚what hastow þouȝt?
130 Tel me soþe, forhele it nouȝt:
Whan þenkestow for to wyve,
Whom and whare? so mot þou þrive'.
‚Sire', he seyde, ‚by seynt Cutberd,
þer nys no womman in midlerd,
135 *For* no þing, men miȝt me crave,
Bot one for soþe, þat ich wolde have
*Loved and se*rved in al my lyve.
(An) *oþer, þan hir*, nyl ich never wyve:
Hir love have ich dere bouȝt.
140 Sir erl, now hastow al my þouȝt.'
    þe erl Rohaut seiþ: ‚sire Guyoun,
Wher is þat may, in what regioun?
Tel me, sire, ich þe biseche,
þe maydenes name, hir faderes eke.'
145 And Guy seiþ: ‚sire, by goddes ore,

                                                        2*

At þis tyme wostow no more.'

þe *erle* takeþ Guy by þe hond

And *seiþ*: ,leve frende, now understonde.

Ich have a douȝter swiþe faire:

150 *Wel* þou wost, heo is myn eire.

(P)*ry þe*, Guy, take hir to wyve:

Half my lond ich wol ȝow ȝive

And al entere after my day:

Ich nave none eir but þat may.'

155 ,Sire', quoþ Guy, ,grant mercy:

Her is a fayre ȝifte sikerly.

þi douȝter lever to me is

In hir smok al one ywis,

þan to wedde wiþ alle Spayne

160 þe emperoures douȝter of Almayne.

The erle hym kist fele siþe

Wiþ gode wille and þonked him swiþe.

,Sir Guy', he seyde, ,ich se by þe,   v^b

Up al þing þou lovest me,

165 Now þou wost my douȝter take

And so many hast forsake.

To day seveniȝt it schal be,

þe spousail, wiþ alle gle

In Warwik, þat cite,

170 Wiþ wel grete solempnite.'

,Sire', quoþ Guy, ,al, þat þou demest:

In alle þing þou me quemest.'

Whan þe tyme was ycome,

þider come many a moder sone,

175 Dukes, erles and knyȝtes many one,

þat to þe spousail were bede echon.

þat maide was diȝt richely,

Wiþ grete worschip hir spoused Guy.

þe bridale þei helden richeliche

180 A fourtenniȝt manschipliche.

Mynstrels many þere were,

Mo never at one fest nere.

þere was harp and tympanie,

Feþele, beme and cymphanie

185 And clerkes wiþ her sautrie,
   þat couþe synge wel myrie.
   Beres and bole ybete þer were
   And apes tumbled in many manere.
   þere was al maner of ₁gle,
190 þat man miȝt þenk oþer se.
   Robes, þat were of riche pris,
   þe panes of veire and of gris,
   þe heiȝe hors, þe grete stede
   þe glemen hadden to her mede.
195 Whan þe fourtenniȝt was gon,
   Ech man hym went þennes home.
   Now haþ Guy al his wille
   Of his lemman boþe loude and stille.
   Fifty dayes to gedere þei were,
200 No day more yfere þei nere.
   It fel in þat first niȝt,
   þat he lay by þat swete wiȝt
   And neiȝhed hir fleschliche,
   A knave child heo conseyved sikerliche.
205 It was in may in someres tyde,
   Guy was at Warwik wiþ pride.
   From huntyng on a day was come,
   Gode plente of venesoun had nome.
   Muche joy he made and solace,
210 So þat in an evenyng, þat myry was,
   Sire Guy to a toure steiȝ
   And lened him to a corner an heiȝ.
   He biheld þe cuntre about ferre,
   þe welkne, þat was wel þik of sterre,
215 And þe weder, was myry and briȝt;
   And Guy þouȝt him anon riȝt . . . .

Dieses Fragment ist am nächsten verwandt mit C, der noch ungedruckten Pergamenthandschrift in Cajus (sprich Key's, d. h., keez) College zu Cambridge, die im Anfange des 15. Jahrhunderts von zwei Händen geschrieben ist (Nr. 107 des Katalogs von Smith). Der Grad der Verwandtschaft wird sich aus zwei verschiedenen Stellen ergeben, die wir vergleichen wollen. Die erste sei der Schluss des Fragmentes von V. 205

an. Doch mag hier zunächst die entsprechende Partie des
französischen Originals stehen und zwar nach der Handschrift
des Corpus Christi College zu Cambridge (L, 6. Fol. 103—182),
die wohl erst im 14., nicht schon, wie der Katalog angibt, im
13. Jahrhundert geschrieben ist. Die betreffende Stelle lautet
Fol. 148ʳ a:

> Ceo fu en mai el tens de esté
> Ke Gui ert en Warewik la cité.
> De berser ert un jor repairé,
> Venesun ad pris a grant plenté.
> 5 Mult joius e lez se feseit:
> A une vespre ke bele esteit
> Gui en une tur mounta,
> En hault as estres se apuia.
> Le pais environ ad esguardé
> 10 E le se[c]l[e] ke tant ert esteilé
> E le tens ke ert seri e cler.
> Gui comence dunc a penser
> Com deus u. s. w.

C gibt nun S. 147 f.:

> It was in may in somers tyde,
> Guy was at Warrewik *in moche* pride.
> From huntyng on a daye *he is* come,
> *Grete* plente of venyson *he hath* nome.
> 5 Moche joye he made and solas,
> So that in *the* evenyng (*so* mery *he* was)
> *The contree he behelde* aboute farre (l. ferre)
> *And* the *skye* thikke *with* sterre
> And the weder, *that* was mery and bright.
> 10 *Guy bethoughte* him anone right,
> That god u. s. w.

Es fehlen hier zwischen 6 und 7 zwei Verse (= 7. 8 O,
wie ich kurz den altfr. Text nennen will, und 211. 212 S),
auch sonst kommen Abweichungen vor, die durch den Druck
bezeichnet sind: diese sind so unbedeutend, dass der Schluss
unvermeidlich ist, dass S und C ein und dieselbe Uebersetzung
repräsentiren.

Sehen wir nun, wie diese Stelle in den übrigen Texten
lautet, zunächst in dem Edinburgher Auchinleck MS. aus der

ersten Hälfte des 14. Jahrhunderts, nach welchem Turnbull die Geschichte von Guy und seinem Sohne Reinbrun (denn so und nicht ‚Rembrun' muss der Name lauten) im Jahre 1840 für den Abbotsford Club herausgegeben hat. Nur ein Theil ist in kurzen Reimpaaren abgefasst, diesen nenne ich A: was in zwölfzeiligen Strophen behandelt ist, bezeichne ich mit α. Wir lesen nun in α (S. 276 bei Turnbull):

20   þan was sir Gy of gret renoun
       And holden lord of mani a toun,
       As prince, proude in pride,
       þat erl Rohaut and sir Gyoun
5   In fretþe to fel þe dere adoun
       On hunting þai gun ride.
       It bifel opon a somers day,
       þat sir Gy at Warwike lay
       (In herd is nouȝt to hide):
10   At niȝt, in tale as it is told,
       To bedde went þe bernes bold
       Bi time to rest þat tide.
21   To a turet sir Gy is went
       And biheld þat firmament,
       þat þicke wiþ steres stode.
       On Jesu u. s. w.

Der Ausdruck 21, 2. 3 α þat firmament, þat *þicke wiþ steres* stode verglichen mit 214 S þe welkne, þat was wel *þik of sterre* und 8 C the skye *thikke with sterre* (= 10 O e le sel ke tant ert esteilé) könnte vermuthen lassen, dass die strophische Bearbeitung nach der uns in SC (natürlich in jüngerer Gestalt) vorliegenden Uebersetzung gemacht ist, doch bedarf dies einer eingehenden Untersuchung, zu der mein Material noch nicht ausreicht.

Ferner ist zu vergleichen Fol. 206ʳ b von c, der ungedruckten Papierhandschrift der Universitätsbibliothek zu Cambridge (Ff, 2, 38) aus dem 15. Jahrhundert. Es heisst da:

       Hyt was in a somers tyde,
       That Gye had moche pryde.
       He came fro huntyng on a day
       With grete solace and mekyll play:
5   þey toke plente of veneson

And broght hyt unto the towne.
At evyn he wente into a towre
Wyth moche yoye and honowre.
He behelde there the ayre
10 And the lande, þat was so fayre:
The wedur was clere and sternes bryʒt.
Guy beganne to thynke ryght,
How god u. s. w.

Wir haben hier ganz dieselbe Anzahl von Versen, wie
in O und S. Zweimal finden wir denselben Reim, wie in S und
C, nämlich tyde : pryde 1.2 c, 205.206 S, 1.2. C und bryʒt:
ryght 11.12 c, 215.216 S, 9.10 C. Doch sind die Verschieden-
heiten zwischen c und SC sonst so bedeutend, dass wir in c
eine zweite selbstständige Uebersetzung des Originals sehen
müssen: jene ganz naheliegenden gleichen Reime können gegen
diese Annahme nicht geltend gemacht werden.

Endlich kommt noch in Betracht d, der von Copland
(nach Ritson vor 1567) gedruckte Text, der auf der Vorderseite von Dd 1 die folgenden Verse enthält:

After it fell upon a day,
As syr Guy came from play,
Into a towre he went on hye
And looked about him farre and nye.
5 Guy stoode and bethought him tho,
How he had done u. s. w.

Der Reim 1.2 day : play stimmt zu 3.4 c, dagegen
erinnert das Reimwort on hye V. 3 an 212 S an heiʒ. Dass
diese Berührungen zufällig sein können, liegt auf der Hand;
dass sie aber wirklich zufällig sind, wird sich im Fortgange
dieser Untersuchung ergeben, wenn es sich herausstellt, dass
d die Modernisirung einer dritten selbstständigen Uebersetzung ist.

Ich gehe jetzt zu einer zweiten Stelle über, die in S die
Verse 23—58 umfasst. Ihnen entsprechen in O (Fol. 147ᵛb
und 148ʳa):

,Sire Gui', fait ele, ,vostre merci!
E ieo veraiement vus di
Ke mult ai requise esté
Des plus riches del regné,

5 Mes amer nul ne voleie
Ne a nul jur ne f(e)reie.
A vus me doin e ottreie (l. ottroi),
Vostre pleisir facez de moi'.
Gui de joie l'en ad baisé[e]
10 Une mes de rien ne fut tant lé.
A sa amie prist puis congié,
Si est a sun ostel alé.
Joie demaine e nuit e jour,
Quant est aseur de s'amur.

Diesen 14 Versen entspricht eine gleiche Anzahl in C
(S. 145 f.):

,Sir Guy', she seide, ,graunt mercy!
And y the sey sikirly,
That y have desired bee
Of the richest of this reigne,
5 And noon to love nas my wille,
Ne never noon love y nelle,
Bot the, to whom y yive me:
To thy wille y shall alweys bee'.
Guy hir kiste: so gladde he was,
10 Nevere more joyefull of noo cas.
At hir than his leeve he nome
And to his inne he wente home.
Nyghte and day he made solas,
Of hir love thoo he siker was.

Eben so viel Verse hat c (Fol. 206ᵛa):

,Syr', sche seyde, ,gramercye!
I yow sey sekerlye,
For me þer hath be preyere
Of kynge and dowke ferre and nere.
5 Of them all wolde y nane:
Ye had my love with yow tane.
I am yowrys (hyt ys skylle)
To do with me at yowre wylle'.
Gye hur kuste wyth yoye than:
10 He was never so gladd a man.
He toke hys leve and home wente:
Of myrthe and yoye was hys entente.

He made yoye nyght and day,
When he was seker of þat maye.

C und c verhalten sich hier ganz so, wie an der zuerst
verglichenen Stelle: sie haben einmal (1.2) den gleichen naheliegenden Reim, aber sonst ist ihnen eben nicht mehr und
nicht minder gemeinsam, als was von zwei selbstständigen,
aber genauen Uebersetzungen zu erwarten ist. In S aber, das
an dieser Stelle einen ganz eigenen Weg wandelt, müssen wir,
wenn wir beide Stellen zugleich ins Auge fassen, eine theil-
weise erweiternde Bearbeitung derselben Uebersetzung erkennen,
die C gibt.

Es bleiben noch α und d übrig. α (Turnbull S. 269) gibt:

6   þan answerd þat swete wiȝt
      And seyd oȝain to him ful riȝt:
      ,Bi him, þat schope mankinne,
      Ich am desired day and niȝt
   5 Of erl, baroun and mani a kniȝt:
      For noþing wil þai blinne.
      Ac Guy‘, sche seyd, ,hende and fre,
      Al mi love is layd on þe:
      Our love schal never tvinne.
 10 And, bot ich have þe to make,
      Oþer lord nil y non take
      For al þis warld to winne‘.

7   Anon to hir þan answerd Gy,
      To fair Felice, þat sat him bi,
      þat semly was of siȝt.
      ,Leman‘, he seyd, ,gramerci!‘
   5 Wiþ joie and wiþ melodi
      He kist þat swete wiȝt.
      þan was he boþe glad and bliþe
      (His joie couþe he noman kiþe)
      For þat bird so briȝt.
 10 He no was never þer biforn
      Half so bliþe, seþe he was born,
      For nouȝt, þat man him hiȝt.

Zur Bestimmung der Quelle von α ergibt diese Stelle,
so viel ich sehe, nichts: auch aus der Fassung von d lässt

sich nichts folgern, doch beachte man die drei sayd (1.3.7)
und daneben noch quod (5).

> ‚Certaynly‘, then sayd Phelis,
> ‚Knight of this worlde moste of pryce,
> On you certes, syr‘, she sayd,
> Over all thing my love is layd.
> 5 For certes, syr,‘ quod she,
> ‚I loved never man so well, as yee;
> And now‘, she sayd, ‚lowde and still
> I will be at your will‘.

Ich will auch nicht unterlassen, auf die gleiche Phrase
6, 8 α und 4 d aufmerksam zu machen: es kann das aber
leicht ein Zufall sein.

Ich habe oben d für die Modernisirung einer dritten
selbstständigen Uebersetzung erklärt. Von dieser gibt es
einige weit ältere Bruchstücke, von denen Sir Thomas Philipps
einen freilich‘nicht ganz vollständigen und nicht fehlerfreien
Abdruck in seiner Privatdruckerei zu Middle Hill 1838 besorgt
hat. In dem Wiederabdrucke von Turnbull (in der Vorrede
zum Guy aus dem Auchinleck MS. XXVIII ff) sind einige
Fehler verbessert und hin und wieder auch ein geringes mehr
mitgetheilt, ohne dass aber dieser die Handschrift selbst gesehen
zu haben scheint. Wahrscheinlich waren diese Verbesserungen
und Ergänzungen in dem Turnbull von Philipps geschenkten
Exemplare des Abdrucks gemacht, während sie das von mir
benutzte des britischen Museums nicht hat. Philipps gibt nicht
an, woher die Handschrift sei; Turnbull bemerkt nur, Philipps
habe die Bruchstücke gedruckt ‚from a MS found in the cover
of an old book‘. In der neuesten von W. Carew Hazlitt be-
sorgten Ausgabe von Thomas Warton’s History of English
Poetry (London 1871) II 162, Anm. 2 heisst es, Turnbull ‚has
printed at length a fragment of an otherwise unknown English
version in the possession of Sir Thomas Philipps‘. Es ist
Hazlitt und seinen Mitarbeitern entgangen, dass sich das Manuscript jetzt wenigstens im britischen Museum befindet. Es ist
Add. MS. 14408 enthaltend Lydgate, De Regimine Principis etc.
‚At the end are 4 leaves on vellum, containing a fragment
of the romance of Guy, Earl of Warwick, in English verse,
which formed the fly leaves of the original binding, written

in a hand of the beginning of the XIV. century‘, wie es im Kataloge heisst. Die Bruchstücke, die ich mit P bezeichnen will (sie bilden jetzt Fol. 74—77), haben in Folge ihrer Verwendung so gelitten, dass sie fast überall schwer und zum Theil gar nicht zu lesen sind.

Auch hier will ich die zur Vergleichung ausgewählte Stelle zuerst im Original geben (131ᵛa):

> E ieo nes poeie mes attendre:
> Sur mun chival ma amie pris,
> Einz el chemin mult tost me mis.
> Mult grant aleure m'en alai,
> 5 Ma bele amie od mei portai.
> Dunc me commencerent a chacer,
> E ieo m'en aloie sur mon destrer.
> Tut cel jur me chacerent,
> Deskes a la nuit unkes ne finerent.
> 10 Passai le pais e les contrées
> · E les muntz e les valées.
> A un' ewe vinc ke mult ert grant:
> De totes parz vindrent siwant.
> Ne poei nef ne pount trover,
> 15 Dunt la rive(re)pusse passer:
> Radde e lée ert la rivere.
> Eschaper ne poeie en autre manere:
> El bon chival mult me afiai,
> En l'ewe me mis, si passai.
> 20 Quant la rivere esteie passé,
> Ester les vi al entrer del gué:
> Mettre dedeinz pas ne se oserent,
> A tant ariere retornerent.
> En ceste forest m'en vinc errant,
> 25 Od mei ma amie suef portant.
> Ne cremoie laron ne robeur,
> Einz quidoie estre asseur.
> Ke de veiller, ke de juner
> E surketut de travailler
> 30 Mult grant somil avoie,
> En ceste place me dormeie.
> Ma amie devant mei seeit,

Mun chival a un raim lié esteit.
A tant survindrent chivalers,
35 Quinze robburs ke mult sunt fiers.
A mort m'unt naufré en dormant:
De la vie ne ai tant ne kant.
Dit vus ai tote ma vie,
Com ieo ai, las, perdu ma amie,
40 Dunt plus me doil ke de ma mort,
Si de lui nen aveie confort.
Mult criem k'elle seit honie
Des robburs ke deus maldie.
Oi avez ma aventure,
45 Ne quid ke a homme avenist si dure.
Ore te conjur par ta fei
Ke tu as ci plevi a mei
Ke tantost com ieo serrai mortz,
Enterrer facez mon cors
50 A abbeie ou a muster,
Ke beste nel pusse devorer;
E ke vus irrez sur cet munt
La où les quinze robburs sunt:
Tuz ensemble les troverez.
55 Si vus occire les porrez,
Comquere i porrez ainz le seir
Ke ne la durr(e)ie pur nul aver,
Ma amie, la vaillante Osille
(Ni ad tant belle deskes en Sezille),
60 E mon chival ke tant est corant:
El mund ni ad un plus vaillant.
Par force en painime le conquis
Del fiz al soldain˙ Salakis.

Dafür gibt P (nach meiner Lesung: vgl. Philipps A,
Turnbull XXVIII f):

. . . . . i moht me na langer defend,
Wiht my lemman gan i wend.
I went away ay god paas,
Riht to nyht thay goun me chas,
5 Til i com at ai water brad:
My hors swam over, i was glad.

Wen thay com thar, thay durst noht pas:
Swa dep that ilk water was.
Bot than torned thay ogayn:
10 My lemman and i went forht alayn.
I wend that nicht sicerlyk
Rest me in thys wod thyk.
Wat for fastyng, wat for wakyng
I fel her doun in slumeryng:
15 My lemman sat byfor me
And my hors bounden by ay tre.
Fiften knythes[1] com in ai stounde,
Al slapand[2] gaf thay me thys wonde.
I mun dye thar[3] of, wol i wate:
20 Swa icham in ivel[4] state.
Of my self ne hys me[5] noht:
On my lemman es al my thoht.
The theves led hyr fra me:
Thuru[6] thaym mun sho honyst be.
25 Nou[7] haf i talde the,[8] sire knyht,
Hou i ham thus ivel dyht.
For that ilke leute,
That to[9] lang are hiht me,
Ger graf me in g : : sted
30 Als sone, als i am ded.
Ga nou up unto : : : : grene,
Thar thaas ilk robbours bene.
Wiht thaym hys my lemman Osile
(Es nan fayrer unto Cisile)
35 And my palfray wiht, als milk:
In this land is nan swilk.

---

[1] Dieses Wort, dass bei genauem Zusehen nicht zu verkennen ist, lautet
bei Philipps und Turnbull koyches, was sinnlos ist.
[2] Richtig ein Wort im MS., dagegen slap, and Ph, slap and T.
[3] thay Ph. u. T.
[4] snel Ph. u. T.
[5] So auch T., aber ne Ph.
[6] Thurn Ph. u. T.
[7] Mon Ph. u. T.
[8] the ist das letzte, was Ph. und T. von diesem Bruchstück geben.
[9] = þou wegen der Anlehnung an That entstellt.

In haythenes i wan hym wyt gret pris
Of the soudans sone ywis.
Diese Stelle lautet in d:
    And when that i might no more fighte,
    With my lemman i rode forth right,
    Till it was night, a good pace,
    And fast after they gan me chase,
 5 Till i came to a water brode:
    I wote not, how long i there abode.
    An arme it was of the sea,
    But gods grace so helpe me,
    That my steede swifte and good
10 Bare us both over the flood.
    There turned they agayne echone,
    For to sue me they durst not one.
    To this forrest fled wee,
    For here we weende seker to have bee.
15 So for honger and long fasting
    I fell downe here in sowning.
    My lemman sate before me,
    My horse was reyned to a tree.
    Fyfteene knightes came in a stound
20 And thus asleepe me can wounde.
    Therefore i wote, i must needes dye:
    So feeble i am withouten lye.
    Robbers all fyfteene they bee,
    My lemman they robbed away fro me.
25 Of my selfe ne charge i nought,
    But on my lemman is all my thought:
    Through them, syr, she might be shent.
    Now haste thou heard˜ all my talent.
    My name‘, he sayd with mylde voyce,
30 ,Is syr Terry of Gurmoyse.
    Some tyme i was holden doughty,
    My father knight erle Anbry‘.
    That sayd Terry: ,for that leawte,
    That thou hightest ever to me,
35 When i am deade, doe me bury
    In some place good and merry.

But yonder upon yon greene
Bene the robbers all fyfteene.
Wyth them is my lemman, fayre Osyle,
40 In much dread and great perrill.
Thou seemest a man of much might:
Speede thee to the robbers right,
That bene yonder upon yon montayne;
For thou mightest her win certayne
45 Or else thou shalt without leasing
Winne thee pryce and other thing,
That thou wouldest not give ywis
For all this world good or blis.
Thou mayst them slea with dint of swearde
50 And win the fayrest mayde of middle erde
And my well renning steede:
In this worlde is no better at neede.
I wan in pany my horse and pryse
Of the soudan Salabrys.

In d sind 16 Verse mehr, als in P: 14 davon sind, wie
die Uebereinstimmung von O und P lehrt, offenbar Zusätze,
nämlich 29—32 d (zwischen 26 und 27 P, 45 und 46 O) und
41—50 d (zwischen 34 und 35 P, 59 und 60 O); ausserdem
aber stehen 5—10 P, also 6 Versen, 5—12 d, also 8, gegen-
über. Abgesehen davon stimmt d mit P ziemlich genau überein,
soweit nicht etwa in d alterthümliche oder nördliche Reime
weggeschafft werden mussten. Das alterthümliche wend 2 P,
ivel dyht 26 P, sted 29 P konnte nicht bleiben, ebensowenig
brad : glad 5.6 P (was brode : glad ergeben hätte), ogayn :
alayn 9.10 P (again : alone), sicerlyk : thyk 11.12 P (sickerly :
thick), wate : state 19.20 P (wot : state), milk : swilk 35.36 P
(milk : such). Wo dagegen die Reime nicht geändert zu werden brauchten, ist die Zusammengehörigkeit von P und d nicht
zu verkennen: 3—5 P = 3—5 d, 13—18 P = 15—20 d, 21—24
P = 23—27 d (wenn auch in anderer Reihenfolge), 27—28
P = 33—34 d, 31—34 P = 37—40 d, 37—38 P = 53—54 d.
Dass aber P keineswegs die directe oder indirecte Quelle von
d war, ergibt sich schon daraus, dass d den Namen Salabrys
wenn auch vielleicht entstellt, erhalten hat, während sich in P
an seiner Stelle ein offenbar unechtes ywis zeigt.

Aber d steht nicht nur mit P im Zusammenhange, sondern auch und zwar in einem viel näheren mit einem älteren Drucke, von dem sich ein Blatt in der Bodlejana (Douce Fragments 20) befindet. Auf dem Umschlag ist von moderner Hand bemerkt: ‚The same type as that used in the fragments of Bevis of Hampton and Robyn Hode, and several other books . . . all of which were certainly printed by Wynkyn de Worde'. Dem Blatte, das ich w nennen will, entspricht in d Ji II und III. Die Abweichungen sind fast nur orthographisch; doch sind auch einige Fehler von w in d nicht vorhanden. Z. B. wenn es in w heisst:

> To Lolbronde he lete it flye,
> But he myghte not so hye,

so gibt d richtig Colbronde und myght not reche. War w die Vorlage von d, so dass die angeführten und sonstige Ver-änderungen in d Coplands Conjecturen wären, oder hatten d und w eine gemeinschaftliche Grundlage? An diese Fragen, die ich nicht beantworten kann, mögen sich gleich noch einige andere schliessen. Gibt das Fragment von 36 Blättern ‚printed in a thinner letter than W. de Worde's', das sich nach Warton (ed. Hazlitt) II, 162 im Besitze von Mr. Staunton of Longbridge House, co. Warw., befindet und von Pynson herrühren soll — gibt dieses denselben Text wie d? Auch Cawood's Ausgabe? Wo ist ein Exemplar von diesen? Wo ein vollständiges Exem-plar von d? Auskunft hierüber wäre mir sehr erwünscht.

Es bleibt jetzt noch zu beweisen, das Pd wirklich eine dritte selbstständige Uebersetzung repräsentiren. Die erste ist nun an dieser Stelle nicht nur durch C, sondern auch durch das weit ältere A vertreten. Ich gebe den entsprechenden Abschnitt nach A, die Abweichungen von C aber, soweit sie nicht bloss, wie man sich nicht ganz genau auszudrücken pflegt, orthographischer Natur sind, in den Anmerkungen, wodurch zugleich die Zusammengehörigkeit von A und C bewiesen wird. [1]
Turnbull S. 164 f. (V. 4233 ff.) = C 118 f.

---

[1] Es hätte daher in Warton (ed. Hazlitt) II, 28, wo vom Auchinleck MS. die Rede ist, und nicht 32, wo c angeführt ist, hinzugefügt werden sollen: ‚Another copy at Caius College, Cambridge'.

Ich toke mi leman on mi stede
And over þat water wiþ hir ich ȝede.
Alle þat day þai driven me,
Alle fort þai no miȝt for niȝt yse.
5 When y was passed þe river, ariȝt
In hert y was glad and liȝt.
þat water passi þai no durstin,
þan owayward turn þai mostin.
In þis forest y come rideinde,
10 Bifor me mi leman ledeinde.
Y no dred robours no þef non,
Ac al siker ich wende forþ gon.
What of wakeing and of fasting
And eke þat oþer treveyling
15 Osleped swiþe sore ich was
And lay and slepe in þis plas.
þan com fiftene outlawes strong
Wiþ her men and here me afong:
Alle slepende þai wounded me.
20 Anon riȝt nomen he
Mi leman: þai han hir ladde fro me.
Now, sir, take þerof pite.
Bi þe treuþe, þou hast me pliȝt,
Socour mi leman, ȝif þou miȝt.
25 And, when þat ich dede be,
Do me biry, ich bidde þe.
To þat hulle þou wende anon:
þou hem findes þer ichon;
And ȝif þat þou so miȝti be,
30 þatow may hem alle sle,
Winne þou miȝt a maiden fre:
In þe warld may non feirer be.
And ȝete y may þe more telle:
Mi stede þai han, þat is so snelle,
35 þat wiþ strengþe in peyneme ich wan
Of Solagimis, þe sone soudan.

1 upon. 4 Tyll they for nyghte might noo lenger see. 5.6 *fehlen.* 8 oway-
ward] ayene. 9 So into this. 10 guyding. 11 robboure. 12 sure. forþ] to have.
13 of] for *beidemal.* 14 And for other grete traveilling. 15 Forsleped. 16 And

felle aslepe. 17 come here. 18 and gan me fonge. 19 thus they. 20 And than forsothe y telle the. 21 They toke my lemman and ledde hir with theim. 22 For goddes love, sire, have pitee nowe then. 23 For the. 26 Thou doo. pray. 28 There shalt thou fynde the outlawes echoon. 29 And, sir, yf thou so good bee. 30 might. 32 noon fairer may. 33—36 *fehlen*.

Es kann nicht dem geringsten Zweifel unterliegen, dass hier in AC eine andere Uebersetzung erhalten ist, als in Pd. Endlich bleibt noch c (Fol. 189ʳb):

> I myght not defende me than.
> Y toke my lemman me behynde
> . And rode forthe, as the wynde.
> They chasyd me that ylke day:
> 5 Fro the stedde y wanne a way.
> Tyll hyt came to darke nyght,
> Evyn they folowed me ryght.
> All þat londe thorowe y rode,
> Tyll y cam to a watur brode.
> 10 Schyppe myght y there fynde none.
> They chasyd þedur everychone.
> Brode and depe the watur was,
> And odur wey myght y not passe.
> I hastyd me upon my stede,
> 15 That was gode at every nede.
> The watur y toke and passyd wele
> Wyth goddys grace every dele.
> Forthe y wente a gode pase:
> Ther durste noman come, þere y was.
> 20 Hedur y cam to thys foreste
> Wyth my lemman, y loved beste.
> I wente, none had be in þys wode,
> That wolde have done me but gode.
> What for wakyng and for fastynge,
> 25 What for travell and for fyghtynge
> I restyd me on thys grownde
> (And felle aslepe in a stownde)
> And tyed my hors tyll a tre:
> My lemman sate before me.
> ·30 Then came thevys fyftene,
> Bolde men and eke kene.

All slepynge þey woundyd me:
I am dedd, as thou mayste see.
Sythen þey toke Oʒelde, þat maye,
35 And my stede and wente awaye.
I have þe tolde now all my lyfe,
How y have bene in mekyll stryfe.
Of the dethe geve y noght:
On þat maye ys all my thoght.
40 Of þe thevys she getyþ grete shame.
God venge me for hys holy name.
Thou haste harde now my care.
I wot, y may leve no mare.
Yn goddys name y conyure the,
45 That þy trowþe þou plyght to me:
As soone, as þat y am dedd,
Thou bere me to some gode stedd,
To churche or to abbaye,
Or y be any wylde bestus praye.
50 To þe ʒondur hylle, loke, þat þou fare,
And the thevys þou shalt fynde þare.
Yf þou myght þem confownde
And þe thevys brynge to grownde,
Thou mayste wynne to þyn honde
55 The fayrest maydyn in þys londe
And also the beste stede,
That ever knyght rode on at nede:
Y wan hym in paynymlonde
Owt of a Sarsyns honde.

Auch c hat, wie man sieht, keine nähere Beziehung zu Pd: die Uebereinstimmung von 38.39 c mit 21.22 P, 25.26 d und 57.58 c mit 51.52 d erklärt sich hinlänglich aus der Formelhaftigkeit solcher Ausdrücke.

Wir haben nach alledem also, so viel ich dies bis jetzt beurtheilen kann, drei selbstständige me. Uebersetzungen des altfranzösischen Guy zu unterscheiden.

Die erste liegt vor in A, C, S: ob die Bearbeitung α auf dieser beruht oder auf einer andern oder auf dem Original bleibt noch zu ermitteln.

Die zweite ist nur in c vertreten.

Die d r i t t e liegt zu Grunde P, w, d; ob auch den oben
erwähnten beiden mir unbekannten Drucken, bleibt abzuwarten.

2. Lydgate's Leben des Guy von Warwick.

Lydgate's Leben des Guy von Warwick ist, soviel bisher
bekannt ist, nur ein einziges Mal überliefert, nämlich in einer
Pergamenthandschrift aus der ersten Hälfte des fünfzehnten
Jahrhunderts auf der Bodlejana zu Oxford, Laud. 683 (D 31),
Fol. 65ʳ—78ʳ. Die Verse sind abgesetzt, der Anfang der Strophen
durch bunte grosse Buchstaben bezeichnet; sonst stehen am
Versanfange in der Regel gewöhnliche Buchstaben. Jede Seite
enthält nur eine einzige Spalte Schrift in 21—27 Zeilen. Die
Hand ist deutlich, doch u und n, st und ft sind nicht zu unterscheiden. Die Haken, die regelmässig auslautendem g, k, t, f
angehängt, und die Striche, die häufig durch den Hals von h
gezogen sind, halte ich für blosse Verzierung: deshalb lässt
sie der Abdruck, den ich nach meiner eigenen Abschrift gebe,
unberücksichtigt.

Ich sagte oben, das Werk sei nur einmal überliefert.
Bei Warton (ed. Hazlitt) II, 32 heisst es allerdings: ‚Copies
of Lydgate's translation are in the Bodleian, and in Harleian
MS. 5243‘. Allein diese Handschrift des britischen Museums
enthält (vgl. Turnbull in der Vorrede seiner Ausgabe des Guy
XXV ff.): ‚The corrected historie of S i r G w y, E a r l e of
W a r w i c k, surnamed the H e r e m i t e; begun by D o n L i d g a t e
monck of st. E d m u n d e s B e r y e; but now dilligentlie exqui-
red from all A n t i q u i t i e, by J o h n L a n e. 1621.‘ Am Schlusse
der Handschrift liest man: ‚Finis John Lane‘. Darauf
‚The licence.

This poem containinge a corrected historie of G u y E a r l e
o f W a r w i c k in 87 leaves of large quarto, written by mʳ J o h n
L a n e hath licence to ‘bee printed. Jul: 13⁰ 1617.
John Tauerner
as in the original‘.

Es ist dies also nicht Lydgate's, sondern John Lane's
Guy of Warwick, den Edward Philips, Milton's Neffe, in
seinem Theatrum Poetarum (ed. Brydges 318. 319) erwähnt.
‚John Lane‘, heisst es da, ‚a fine old Queen Elizabeth's gentle-

man, who was living within my remembrance, and whose several
Poems, had they not had the ill fate to remain unpublisht,
when much better meriting than many, that are in print, might
possibly have gained him a name not much inferior, if not
equal to Drayton, and others of the next rank to Spenser, but
they are all to be produc't in manuscript, namely his ‚Poetical
Vision‘, his ‚Alarm to the Poets‘, his ‚Twelve Months‘, his
‚Guy of Warwick, a Heroic Poem‘ (at least as much as
many others that are so entitled), and lastly his ‚Supplement
to Chaucer's Squire's Tale.‘

Warton fand das zuletzt erwähnte Werk im Ashmolean
Museum zu Oxford und spricht darüber in seinen Observations
on Spenser I 155 f: ‚I conceived great expectations of him on
reading Philips' account. But I was greatly disappointed, for
Lane's performance, upon perusal, proved to be not only an
inartificial imitation of Chaucer's manner, but a weak effort
of invention‘. Dazu bemerkt Nathan Drake in Shakespeare
and his Times (Pariser Ausgabe 1843 S. 326): ‚This discovery,
however, should not arrest all future research; for his four
preceding poems . . . may yet warrant the decision of Philips‘.

Ich fürchte aber, dass auch ein Leser von Lane's Guy
Philips' Urtheil zu günstig finden muss. Ich selbst hatte, wie
ich aufrichtig gestehen muss, nicht Zeit und Lust, mich durch
die gesammten 26 Cantos auf mehr denn einem halben Tausend
Spalten von über 30 Zeilen durchzuwinden. Ich begnügte mich
mit einer Lectüre derjenigen Stellen, an denen sich eine Be-
nützung von Lydgate's Gedicht, wenn sie vorhanden wäre,
zeigen müsste: indessen ich konnte nicht die geringste Spur
einer solchen entdecken. Doch tritt Lydgate selbst in Lane's
Gedicht auf, um sowohl den Prolog als den Epilog zu sprechen.
Fol. 1ʳ heisst es unter der Ueberschrift ‚The Poet Lidgates
Complaint‘:

> Provokd! out of my grave I com on cause,
> To plaine the breach of Allegorick lawes,
> I com, Saint Edmund Buries monck of late,
> Don Chaucers pupil, whoe could declamate
> Of anie notion in own native gwise
> And poetizinge, coold allegorize u. s. w.

Am Schlusse des Prologs erklärt Lydgate:

> My mind I have imparted to my frend,
> Whoe shall my leaves renewe.

Endlich 131ʳ beginnt ‚The Poet Lidgates Epiloge‘ mit dem Verse

> By promise I from cloister com againe.

Nach alledem ergibt John Lane's Guy nichts für die Kritik von Lydgate's Gedicht, vielmehr sind wir dafür allein auf die einzige glücklicherweise gute Handschrift angewiesen. Lydgate nennt sich in dieser selbst als den Verfasser des Gedichtes, indem er 73, 7.8 sagt:

> yif ought be wrong   in metre or in substaunce,
> putteth the wyte   for dulnesse on Lydgate.

Auch seine Quelle gibt er an: nach 72.73 ist sein Gedicht eine Uebersetzung

> out of the latyn   maad by the cronycleer
> callyd of old   Gerard Cornybyence,
> wich wrot the dedis   with gret dilligence
> of them, that wern   in Westsex crowned kynges,
> gretly comendyng   for knyghtly excellence
> Guy of Warwyk   in his famous writynges,
>   Of whos noblesse   ful gret heed he took
> his marcyal name   puttyng in remembraunce
> the XI. chapitle   of his hystoryal book,

also eine Uebertragung des 11. Kapitels der lateinischen Geschichte der westsächsischen Könige von Gerardus Cornubiensis. Dieses Kapitel ist gedruckt bei Hearne, Chronicon Prioratus de Dunstaple p. 825—830 unter dem Titel: ‚Girardi Cornubiensis Historia Guidonis de Warwyke‘ und zwar ‚e cod. MS. vet. in Bibl. Coll. Magd. Oxon. n. 147. fol. 227a.‘ Leider habe ich es versäumt, mir in England, wo ich das Buch in Händen hatte, über Lydgate's Verhalten zu seiner Quelle Notizen zu machen: hier ist es mir nicht zugänglich, so dass ich das für später aufsparen muss.

Für die Bestimmung der Abfassungszeit dürfte sich aus der 8. Strophe etwas ergeben. Es ist da vom Unglück als Strafe für begangene Frevel die Rede: es werden beispielsweise genannt Jerusalem, Ninive, Rom, Karthago, Troja, ausserdem aber Paris:

> Paris in Fraunce   hath bad his part, parde,
> ffor leccherie   and veyn ambucyoun.

Man muss an die Greuel denken, deren Schauplatz Paris in den Kämpfen zwischen den Armagnacs und Bourguignons in dem zweiten Jahrzehnt des 15. Jahrhunderts vor und während des Krieges mit England wiederholt war, namentlich 1411 und 1419 (Schmidt, Geschichte von Frankreich 2, 224 ff. 264 ff.), und an die epidemischen Krankheiten, die es 1412 und 1419 heimsuchten. Deshalb, denke ich, können wir Lydgate's Guy etwa um 1420 setzen.

Von poetischem Werthe kann bei unserem Gedicht von modernem Standpunkt aus, der allerdings für die Beurtheilung alter Werke nicht massgebend sein darf, schwerlich die Rede sein. Eine Ausnahme machen höchstens einige wenige sententiöse oder beschreibende Stellen, obwohl auch diese durchaus nicht originell, wohl aber manierirt sind (11, 1. 31, 2. 32, 1). Sonst tritt uns durchweg gereimte Prosa entgegen, die sich meist äusserst langsam und schwerfällig fortbewegt. An der Schwerfälligkeit ist ganz Verschiedenartiges schuld: zunächst die vielen ‚um es kurz zu sagen‘, ‚um zu schliessen‘ u. dgl.,[1] dann die häufigen Berufungen auf Quellen oder die Quelle[2], die auffälligsten Anakoluthien (s. Anm. zu 1, 8), der Gebrauch absoluter Participialconstructionen um die Rede fortzusetzen[3], die überall sich zeigende Wortfülle u. dgl.

---

[1] Breeffly to telle 15, 3. to speke in generall 54, 6. in this mater fforther to procede 12, 1. as i began, in ordre to proceede 26, 1. to conclude, lyk as i began 11, 6. this mater breefly to conclude 69, 1. to make a fynal ende 18, 8. for short conclusioun 35, 5. 47, 8. 54, 5. as ys rehersed heere 34, 1. as maad is mencioun 54, 2. as ye han herd devyse 68, 1. as ye schall understond 55, 8. lyk as ye shall heere 46, 5.

[2] As seith the cronycleer 1, 3. as myn auctour remembreth in serteyn 6, 7. myn auctour writeth so 63, 1. myn auctour wil nat ffayle 36, 5. as the cronycle breeffly doth compile 36, 1. the cronycle doth expresse 63, 6. in cronycle as i reede 12, 3. in story as i reede 23, 7. 30, 8. in cronycle at leyser who lyst reede 10, 3. in cronycles ye may see 5, 4. as i reede 24, 5. remembred as i reede 48, 1. as the story remembreth by scripture 24, 3. by record of scripture 8, 1. as is remembrid of antyquyte 5, 2. as maad is mencyoun 34, 7.

[3] Z. B. 21 ff. ffounde was no wyght to underfonge themprise of this batayll . . . Herald beyng tho absent to seke . . . Raybourne . . . wich was . . . lad away Ffelyce . . . wepyng . . . born by dyscent to ben hir ffadris hayr hir . . . sone (zu ergänzen being: s. zu 17, 2) to succede . . . Rowaud hir ffader named oon the beste knyht.

Was das Metrische anbelangt, so sind die Strophen, mit deren Ende nicht immer auch der Sinn abschliesst, achtzeilig, wonach die Angabe bei Warton (ed. Hazlitt) III, 134 Anm. zu berichtigen ist. Jede Strophe verwendet drei Reime in der Stellung ababbcbc. Die ganz genauen Reime können stumpf oder klingend sein. Für alle 8 Verse der Strophe gilt dasselbe Schema: eine Cäsur, die klingend oder stumpf sein kann, zerschneidet den Vers in zwei ungleiche Theile: der erste enthält zwei (vgl. die Anm. zu 16, 8), der andere drei Hebungen. Der Auftakt kann bei beiden Vershälften auch zweisilbig sein oder fehlen. Die Hebung besteht manchmal aus zwei durch einfache Consonanten getrennte Silben mit kurzen Vocalen (zu 2, 3). Die Senkung muss einsilbig sein, darf aber auch zwischen hochtonigen Hebungen fehlen (zu 1, 8). Schwebende Betonung zwischen Auftakt und erster Hebung und beim Reime ist öfter anzunehmen (zu 1, 2. 2, 6. 20, 2; vgl. auch zu 67, 3). Auslautendes unbetontes e in mehrsilbigen Wörtern muss in der Regel als stumm gelten.

Here gynneth the lyff off Guy of Warwyk.
By girardus Cornubiensis.

1 Fro Cristis birthe—	complet nyne hundred yeer
twenty and sevene	by computacioun,
kyng Ethelstan,	as seith the cronycleer,
regnyng that tyme	in Brutys Albioun,
5 duryng also	the persecucyoune
of them of Denmark,	wich with myhty honde
rod, brente and slouh	(made noon excepcioun)
by cruel force	thorugh out al this lond — —
2 Spared non ther,	hih nor louh degre,
chirchis, collegis,	but that they bete hem doun,
myhty castellis	and every greet cyte.
in ther ffurie	by ffals oppressioun
5 on to the boundys	of Wynchestre toun
with suerd and feer	they madyn al wast and wylde
and in ther mortalle	persecucyoun

1, 7 die Cäsur, die in der Hs. in der Regel durch zwei senkrechte Striche bezeichnet wird, ist hier sicher hinter slouh und nicht hinter brente, wo das Zeichen steht, anzunehmen: vgl. 2, 8. 6, 8. 13, 2.

spared nat
3 In this brennyng
to Denmark pryncis
lyk woode lyouns
did no favour
5 allas, this lond
froward Fortune
Mars and Mercurie
that bothe þe kyng
4 By froward force
thes danyssh pryncis
on hih hilles
(fortune of werre
5 the peple robbed
for verray dreed
whan the stremys
lyk a gret ryver
5 Paraventure
as is remembrid
of o persone
myhte be withdrawe:
5 reed, how þe myhty
was put a bak
the theffte of Nachor
out of the ffeld
6 Thus by the pryde
and cruel ffurie
this rewm almost
(the swerd of Bellona
5 lordis wer pensiff,
oon of thes tirauntys
and, as myn auctour
the tother was
7 This myscheff wers,
god with his punsshyng
suerd of a tyraunt
with ffurious hand

women greet with chylde.   16
and ffurious cruelte
pompous and elat
void of alle pite
to louh nor hih estaat.   20
stood so dysconsolaat!
hath at hem so dysdeyned,
wer with hem at debaat,
and pryncis wer distreyned   24
to take hem to the fflyght.
ageyn hem wer so wood:
ther ffyres gaff suych lyght
in suych disjoynt tho stood),   28
and spoiled of ther good
of colour ded and pale,
ran doun of red blood
fro mounteyns to þe vale,   32
for sum olde trespace,
of antyquyte,
hap, ffortune and grace
in cronycles ye may see,   36
ffamous Josue
thre dayes in bataylle;
made Israelle to ffle
and in ther conquest faile. 40
and veyn ambycioun
of thes pryncis tweyne
brouht to destruccyoun
gan at hem so disdeyne)   44
þe porail gan compleyne.
callid Anelaphus
remembreth in serteyn,
named Genaphelus.   48
than strok of pestilence —
is ffounde mercyable:
punssheth with vyolence,
mortalle and vengable.   52

2, 8 Cäsur hinter women Hs. 3, 1 and fehlt, vgl. 12, 7.
6, 8 Cäsur nach named Hs.

5 wher folk repente,
that sit above,
but thes tirauntys
with suerd and flawme
8 God ffor synne
hath chastysed
and suffred hem
record Jerusalem,
5 Paris in Fraunce
ffor leccherie
palpable examples
of Rome, Cartage
9 This mater offte
for lak of wisdam
that peplys hertys
to sue vertu,
5 wynd of glad fortune
for ther dismeritees
outrage and vices
thouh kyng Ethelstan
10 Cruell Danys —
ther swerd was wheet
zit, in cronycle
kyng Ethelstan
5 though for a tyme
of his noblesse
the hand of god
to chaunge his trouble
11 The sonne is hatter
the glade morwe
affter wynter
and affter mystys
5 affter trouble
and to conclude,
god lyst to caste
up on his knyght
12 In this mater
constreynt of werre
made hym to drawe,

the lord is ay tretable,
wich halt all in his hond:
to scheden blood most able
troubled al this londe.   56
by record of scripture
many a greet cyte
gret myschef to endure.
record on Nynyvee;   60
hath had his part, parde,
and veyn ambucyoun;
at eye men may see
and of Troie toun.   64
hath been exempleffyede:
and of good consaylle
wer nat ffull applyede
for ther owne avaylle   68
bleuh nat in ther saille:
god punshed hem of right.
hath vengaunce at his taylle.
was a manly knyght,   72
inglysh blood to scheede
and ther ffyres lyght:
at leyser who lyst reede,
was a full noble knyght,   76
eclypsed was his lyght
and royalle mageste.
stoode alway in his myght
in to prosperyte.   80
affter sharpe schours,
ffolweth the dirke nyght,
cometh may with fresshe flours
Phebus schyneth bright,   84
hertys be maade lyght,
lyk as i began:
his mercyable syght
the fforseide Ethelstan.   88
fforther to procede:
and gret adversyte
in cronycle as i reede,

with alle his lordis
5 to have a counsayll
som remedye
ageyn the malys
wrouht by the Danys
13 Off al the lond
remedyo
pryncys, barouns,
in that cyte
5 hap and ffortune
ther hope turned
knyghthood of armes
so destitute
14 In that party
redres to ffynde
Mars set a bak
thus stood the lond
5 strong wer the Danys
kyng Ethelstan
held with his lordis
to ffynde a mene
15 By grace of god
recure to ffynde
breeffly to telle:
benbassatrie
5 streyghtly driven
the kyng of Denmark
or under tribute
as a sojet,
16 Or ellis pleynly
kyng Ethelstan
with Colybrond
day assigned
5 ffor to darreyne
who shal rejoisshe
to holde a septre
and have poscessioun
17 The kyng, the lordis

of hih and louhe degre   72
at Wynchestre the cyte
in all haste to provyde
and ffurious cruelte
in ther marcyal pride.   96
gadryd were the statys
to schapen in this mateere:
bysshopis and prelatys
assembled wern in ffeere.   100
schewyd hem hevy cheere,
to dysesperaunce.
had lost the maneere:
they were of spere and launce.   104
was no remedye,
nor consolacyoun.
all ther chevalrye:
in desolacyoun.   108
proud by ambucioun.
by constreynt and distresse
a counsayll in that toun
his myschef to redresse,   112
how this myht ben amendyd
of ther adversyte.
they were thus condescendyd
or mene of som tretee   116
off necessyte
with homage for to queme
to have this liberte,
rejoysshe his dyademe,   120
of partyes covenaunt
for hym to ffynde a knyght
of Denmark, the geaunt,
to entre with hym in ffyght   124
atween hem to the right,
with strong and myhty hond
by manhood and by myght
in quyete of this londe;   128
beyng there present

13, 2 Cäsur hinter schapen Hs.

with oute respight
to yeve answere
how they list quyte hem
5 outher to make
of septre and crowne,
as i seyde erst,
geyn Colybrond
18 The Denmark dukis
woode and wylful
in outher wise
requyred in haste
5 to have answere
of this convencioun
how they caste hem,
the lyff of tweyn'e
19 This apoyntement
of ffurious haste
kyng Ethelstan
and alle his pryncis
5 affore Wynchestre
the kyng with ínne
and weel þe more,
in his dyffence
20 Knew no bet mene
redres to ffynde
than by assent
he and his lordis,
5 pore and riche,
alle attonys,
with salte teris
by penaunce doyng
21 From hih estatys
of alle degrees
to underfonge
ageyn the geaunt
5 Herald of Harderne,
callid in his tyme

or long dylacyoune
of ther ffynall entent,
(for short conclusioun),   132
a resygnacyoun
outher to ffynde a knyht,
to be ther champioun,
to entryn in to ffight.   134
of malys importable,
in ther marcyal rage
lyst nat be tretable,
benbassat or massage   140
or pleggis for hostage
relacioun to sende,
to puttyn in morgage
(to make a fynal ende).   144
so streitly was forth lad:
they wolde have no delay.
so hard was bestad
put in gret affray.   148
the proude dukis lay,
astoned in his minde
because he knew no way
a champioun to ffynde.   152
as in this mateer
to resoun accordyng,
to taken hym to prayeer,
to wakyng and ffastyng,   156
with oute more taryng:
as they wern off degre,
resembled in ther wepyng
to folk of Nynyvee.   160
doun to the porayll
ffounde was no wyght
themprise of this batayll
of Denmark ffor to ffight   164
þe noble famous knyht,
of prowesse nyh and ferre

17, 2 long] lond oder loud. 17, 4 quyten: vgl. 18, 7.
19, 6 mende.

ffader in armes,
next Guy of Warwyk,
22 This seide Herald
out of this rewm
callid Raynbourne
and alle þe provyncis,
5 wich in yong age
by straunge marchauntis,
Ffelyce his moder
ffor his absence
23 Born by dyscent
hir yonge sone
(in hir tyme
callid the example
5 Rowaud hir ffader
erl of Warwyk,
that was tho dayes,
but he, allas,
24 Paide his dette
by Parcas sustren
and, as the story
whan that Ffelyce
5 by seyde Guy,
he lyk a pilgrym
the nexte morwe
and spedde hym forth
25 Forsook the world
of hih perfeccyoun
lefft wyff and kyn
whom for to serve
5 content with lytel
in worldly pompe
callyng ageyn
kyng Ethelstan
26 As i began,
of his compleynt
not clad in purpil

in every manbis sight
in manhood lodesterre — 168
beyng tho absent
to seke the sone of Guy
in contrees adjacent
that stoode faste by, 172
was stole traytourly
ongoodly lad away
wepyng tendirly
compleynyng nyht and day 176
to ben hir ffadris hayr
Raynborne to succede
was holde noon so ffayr),
of trouthe and womanhede 180
for noblesse and manheede,
named oon the beste knyht,
in story as i reede,
flouryng in hys myht 184
of deth on to nature:
was sponne his lyves threede.
remembreth by scripture,
conseyved hadde in deede 188
sone affter, as i reede,
endewed with all vertu
chaunged hath his weede
for love of Crist Jesu. 192
onknowe to every wight
to leven in penaunce,
and bekam goddis knyght,
was set all his plesaunce: 196
(Crist was his suffysaunce)
he lyst not to sojourne.
on to remembraunce
my penne i wyll retourne, 200
in ordre to proceede
to make mencyoun:
(but chaunged hath his weede),

25, 5 with, wie gewöhnlich, wt geschrieben, aber das t ist nicht ganz vollständig.

blak for mornyng
5 because there was
ffounde no persone
to god above
bespreynt with teris
27 ,O lord', quod he,
cast doun thyn erys
remembre nat
but fro my synnes
5 disespeired
to lese my kyngdam,
but medyacioun
be gracious mene
28 My feith, myn hope,
all hoolly restith
my sheeld, my sheltroun,
be blont and feble,
5 but grace with mercy
thorgh þy support,
while Ethelstan
or he was war,
29 For wach and trouble
devoutly knelyng
the lord above,
that asketh grace
5 for his servaunt
which of his goodnesse
bad hym nat dreede,
wich of his mercy
30 Toward the kyng
bad hym truste
by a tookene
which shal þe schewed
5 of sleep adawed
marked every thyng
to whom the angel
these wordis hadde,
31 ,From the voide
whan Aurora

and desolacyoun,   704
in all his regyoun
his quarell to dyffende,
seyde this orysoun
his grace doun to sende.   208
,of moost magnyfycence,
un to my prayeere.
up on my greet offence,
turne away thy cheere   212
stonding in doubyll were
septre and regalye,
of thy moder deere
to save my partye.   216
my trust, myn affyaunce
in thy proteccyoun:
my suerd and eek my launce
my power is bore doun.   220
list be my champioun
my foon shal me encombre.'
seyde this orysoun,
he ffyll in to a slombre   224
lay in an agonye
by his beddys syde.
wich can no man denye,
with meeknesse void of pride,   228
lyst gracyously provyde;
sente an aungel doun,
but set al ffeer a syde;
had herd his orysoun.   232
cast his look benygne,
al hoolly in his grace
and an entyeer signe,
to hym in riht short space.   236
the kyng lefft up his fface,
and prudently took heede;
his hevynesse tenchasc
in story as i reede: 244
al dyspeir ande dreede.
shewith hir pale light,

to morwen erly
for Crist Jesu
5 to thy requeste
trust up on hym
he shall conserve
thy roiall tytle;
32 At Phebus upriste
whan silver deuh
make thy passage
or that the sonne
5 hath on the levys
abide there meekly,
ffyrst among pore
entrete hym goodly
33 Clad, as a pilgrym,
old and forgrowe
marke hym weell
at thy requeste
5 to accomplysshe
(trust on hym weell)
with goddis myht
in this mater
34 The woordis seid,
on to the kyng
the aungell dyd
and Ethelstan
5 gaff thank to god
neuly rejoisshed
with too bisshopis,
and erlis tweyne
35 Thankyng the lord
as he was bounde
with his bisshopis
at thilke party
5 lyk as the aungell
had told the hour
whan poore ffolk
hadde in costom
36 As the cronycle

arys and take good heede;
of his gracyous myght   244
hath cast doun his sight.
and in þy trust be stable:
of equyte and ryght
ffor he ys mercyable.   248
(set no lenger date),
doth on the fflours ffleete,
toward the north gate,
with his ffervent heete   252
dryed up tho weete.
and god shal to the sende
a pilgrym thou shalt meete:
thy quarell to dyffende.   256
in a brood sclaveyn,
amongys the porayll
and be riht well serteyn,
that he schall nat ffayll   260
manly thy batayll
and for thy purpartye
that he schall prevayll,
thyn axing nat denye'.   264
as ys rehersed heere,
by revelacyoun
onwarly dysapeere,
of greet devossioun   268
off this avysioun.
out off all hevynesse
as maad ys mencyoun,
forth he gan hym dresse   272
of his benygne graunt,
of humble affcccyoun,
and erlys exspectaunt
northward of the toun,   276
(for short conclusioun)
on to the kyng but late,
ffor sustentacyoune
to entren at the gate,   280
breeffly doth compile,

unto purpos
of John Baptyst
how Guy of Warwik
5 at Portysmouth
in his writyng
by grace of god,
tellith, how Guy
37 Whan briht Phebus
on hillis hih
erly on morwe
dried up the deuh,
5 whan seide Guy,
repeired was
fro Portysmouth
to Wynchestre
38 By grace of god,
Guy was hom sent
here taccomplisshe
the laste empryse
5 he ffor to be
onknowe of alle.
to hym was maad
of his requestis,
39 They told hym firste
Harald of Harderne,
was goon to seke
gretly desired
5 wich by discent
by tytle of Ffelyce
at his repair
erl of Warwyk
40 They told hym also
tween them of Denmark
and how that Rowaud,
old erl of Warwik,
5 was ded also;
of hih prudence
lyk a pilgrym

maketh rehersayll,
affore in the vygyle
maad his arryvaylle   284
(myn auctour wil nat ffayle
assignyng hour and tyme)
wich may most avaylle;
evene at the hour of pryme,   288
with his gold tressed bemys
gan shewe his hevenly lyght
and with his hoote stremys
as perlis, silver bright,   292
the noble famous knyght,
from his long pylgrymage,
took his weye right
holdyng his vyage.   296
i deeme trewly,
in to thys regyoun
in knyghthood ffynally
of his hih renoun   300
the kyngys champioun
but, whan he cam to lond,
pleyn relacyoun
how it did stond.   304
in ordre ceryously,
that was so good a knyht,
Raynbourne, the sone of Guy,
of every maner wight,   308
was born of verray right
famous in womanhede
with grace of Cristis myght
justly to succede.   312
of the grete stryff
and Ethelstan þe kyng,
fader to hys wyff,
ful notable of levyng   316
and Guy herd every thyng,
kept hym silff clos:
his leve there takyng

39, 2 of fehlt.   39, 3 Raynbourne fehlt.

goth to Wynchestre
41 Guy took his loggyng,
    with pore men
    wery of travayl
    too hundrid pas
5 where stondeth now
    the nexte morwe
    (god was his guyde
    mong pore men
42 To the north gate,
    by resemblaunce
    as David whilom
    to helpen Saul
5 so for reffuge
    bothe of the kyng
    Guy was provided
    ageyn the pompe
43 By his habite
    thilke tyme
    of whos array
    sauh, goddis promys
5 took up his herte
    god faileth never
    with wepyng teris
    for verray gladnesse
44 Besekyng hym
    with sobbyng cheer,
    to underfonge
    ffor goddys sake
5 to do socour
    in his dyffence
    geyn Colybrond
    for his party
45 Guy wonder sad
    ffeynt and wery
    made his excuse,
    and out of ews
5 ,my wil', quod he,
    the cruell ire

anoon, as he aroos.   320
whan it drouh to nyht,
at an old hospytall
onknowe to every wight
with oute the north wall,   324
a menstre ful roiall.
anoon, as Guy awook
in especyall),
the riht weie he took   328
as grace did hym guye,
so entryng in to toun,
cam ageyn Golye
by grace of god sent doun: 332
and ffor savacyoun
and of al this lond
to be ther champioun
off proude Colybrond   336
and his pylgrym weede
clad in a round sclaveyn;
whan the kyng took heede,
was nat maad in veyn,   340
and knew riht weel serteyn,
his frend on see nor lond.
his chekis spreynt lik reyn
he took Guy by þe hond   344
in moost louly wyse
that routhe was to see,
this knyhtly hih empryse
and mercyfull pyte,   348
in this necessyte,
that he wyll nat ffayll
his champioun for to be,
darreyne the batayll.   352
of look and of vysage,
and dulled of travayll
that he was falle in age
more to be clad in mayll.   356
,yif it myhte avayll
of Danys to appeese,

ffor comoun profit
my lyf inparte
46 The kyng, the lordys
to this pylgrym
Guy for to doon
ffor Jesus sake
5 ys condescendyd,
with goddys grace
as the convencyoun
at place assigned
47 Off this empryse
this convencyoun
tyme set of Jule
place assigned
5 the accord rehersed,
doubylnesse
as the partyes
(for short conclusioun)
48 With oute the gate,
the place callyd
in inglyssh tonge
or ellis Denmark
5 meetyng to gedre
terryble strokys
sparklys . . . .
that to beholde
49 The old pylgrym
spared nat
on his lefft shulder
undir the bordour
5 a streem of blood
the geaunt wood,
thoughte, it sholde
that Guyes suerd
50 Whan Danys sauh,
they cauhte a maner
Guy lyk a knyght
requered manly

good wil shal nat ffayll
to set thys lond in ese.'   360
made greet instaunce
with language and prayere.
un to the kyng plesaunce
and for his moder deere   364
lyk as ye shall heere,
affter the covenaunt,
justly doth requere,
to mete the geaunt.   368
was maad no long delay,
pleynly to darreyne
up on the XII. day,
and meetyng of thes tweyne,   372
the statute and the peyne,
and ffraude set a syde,
were boundyn in serteyn
ther by to abyde.   376
remembred as i reede,
of antyquyte
named Hyde meede
nat fer from the cyte   380
there men myghte see
lyk the dent of thonder,
out off ther harnoys fflee:
it was a verray wonder.   384
quyt hym lyk a knyght,
the geaunt to assayle:
smet at hym with suych myght
of his aventayll,   388
gan by his sydes rayll.
this hydous Colybrond,
gretly hym avayll,
was broke out of his hond.   392
Guy had lost his suerd,
consolacyoun.
in herte nat afferd
of the champioun,   396

48, 7 hinter oder vor sparklys muss etwas fehlen.

5 sith he of wepnys
  to graunte hym oon
  but Colybrond
  to his requeste
51 For he was set
  to execute
  and, while that he
  all attonys
5 cauhte a pollex,
  smette the geaunt
  made his strok
  that his lefft arme
52 With wich strok
  (al his armure
  stoupyng a syde
  to take a suerd,
5 god and grace
  to put his name
  fleib with his ax,
  of the geaunt
53 This thyng accomplisshed
  and by the prowesse
  they of Denmark,
  han crossed sail
5 toward ther cuntre
  ther surquedrye
  kyng Ethelstan
  hadde of Denmark
54 Ther froward pompe
  by Guy of Warwyk,
  the kyng, the clergye
  pryncys, barouns
5 with al the comounte
  hih and lowe
  hym to conveie
  on to ther chirche
55 This seyde Guy
  with gret meknesse

hadde so gret foysoun,
that hour in his diffence.
of indyngnacyoun
gaff noon audyence;   ४ ७॰
on malys and on wrak,
his purpos set on pryde.
and Guy to gedre spak,
Guy sterte out a syde,   ४ ० ४
lyst no lenger byde,
evene in the firste wounde,
so myghtyly to glyde,
and shuldir ffyll to grounde;   ४ ० ॰
the geaunt Colybrond
and body was maad reed)
gan reche forth his hond
wher of Guy took heed.   ४ १ २
that day gaff hym suych speed
ever affter in memorie:
smet of the sturdy heed
and hadde of hym vyctorye.   ४ १ ४
by grace of goddis hond
of Guy, this noble knyght,
as the statute bond,
and take ther weye right   ४ १ ॰
nouther glad nor light
and ther pompe oppressed:
by grace of goddys myht
the pompe ful repressed.   ४ २ ४
with meknesse was repressed
as maad is mencioun,
devoutly have hem dressed,
and burgeis of the toun   ४ २ ॰
(for short conclusioun),
(to speke in generall)
with proscessioun
callyd cathedrall.   ४ ३ २
ther knelyng on his kne
made his oblacioune

52, 2 hoody   53, 6 surquedye.

of thilke ex,
hadde of Danys
5 wich instrument
is yit callid
kept among men
in the vestiarie,
56 Whan al was doon
Guy in al haste
lyk a pilgrym
the kyng ful goodly
5 that he myhte
of this pilgrym
in secre wyse
what was his name,
57 ‚Sertys‘, quod Guy,
touchyng your askyng
beth nat besy
in your desire
5 (to myn excuse
for i shal never
but under bond
assauraunce maad
58 Alle your pryncys
sool be our silff
noon, but we tweyne,
with trouthe assured,
5 duryng my lyf
to no persone
of ffeith and oth),
that ye shall never
59 This thyng contermed
passed the subbarbys
at a cros,
ful devoutly
5 to sette a syde
‚my lord‘, quod he
your lygeman
Guy of Warwyk
60 The kyng astoned

with wich afforn that he
slayn the champioune;   436
thorugh al this regyoun
the ex of Colybrond
of relygyoune
as ye schall understond.   440
(ther is no more to seyne),
caste of hys armure,
put on his sclaveyn.
affter dyd his cure,   444
the grace so recure
to tellyn and nat spare,
to tellyn his aventure,
pleynly to declare.   448
‚ye must have me excused
and your petycioun:
and lat no more be mused
for noon occasioun   452
i have ful greet resoun);
dyscure this mateer,
of a condycyoun,
tween yow and me in feere: 456
avoided by absence,
out of this cyte,
beyng in presence
that ye shal be secre   460
(ye gete no more of me)
(i aske no more avayll
to hih nor louh degre
dyscure my counsayll‘.   464
by proms ful roiall
and boundys of the toun.
that stood ffeer ffrom the wall
the pilgrym knelith doun   468
all suspecyounc.
‚of feith with outen blame
of humble affeccyoune:
trewly is my name‘.   472
gan chaunge cher and face

and in maner
and al attonys
in bothe this armes
5 with offte kyssyng
with grete proffres
of gold, of tresour
with inne his paleys
61 Alle thes profres
and to the kynges
hym recomaundyng
at his departyng
5 with pitous wepyng
un to the kyng
,duryng my lyf
schall i never
62 At ther departyng
sweem of ther speche
the kyng goth hom,
toward Warwyk,
5 no man of hym
where day be day
ffedde poore folk
to praie for hir
63 Thrittene in noumbre:
Guy at his comyng
thre daies space
that took almesse,
5 thankyng the contesse
nat fer fro Warwyk,
of aventure
where he fond on
64 To hym he drouh
for a tyme
the same hermyte
by deth is passed
5 affter whos day
space of too yeer
dauntyng his flessh

63, 1 my.

gan wepyn for gladnesse
he gan hym to enbrace
of royall gentylnesse   476
of ffeithfull kyndenesse,
on the tother syde
and of gret rychesse,
yif he wolde abyde.   480
meekly he forsook
royall mageste
anoon his weie he took.
this avouh maad he   484
knelyng on his kne
in ffull humble entent:
(it may noon other bee)
doon of this garnement'.   488
was but smal langage:
made interupcyoune.
Guy took his vyage
his castell and his toun,   492
havyng suspecyoun,
Ffelyce, his trewe wyf,
of greet devocyoun
and for hir lordys lyf   496
myn auctour writeth so.
forgrowe in his vysage,
he was oon of tho,
with humble and louh corage.   500
in haste took his viage:
the cronycle doth expresse,
kam to an hermytage,
dwellyng in wyldirnesse.   504
besechyng hym of grace
to holde there sojour.
with inne a lytel space
the ffyn of his labour;   508
Guy was his successour
by grace of Cryst Jesu
by penaunce and rigour,

ay more and more   encresyng in vertu.   512
65 God made hym knowe   the day, he sholde deie,
thorugh his moost gracyous   vysytacyoun
be an angel   hys spirit to conveye
affter his bodyly   resolucyoun   516
5 ffor his merites   to the hevenly mansioun.
affter he sente   in haste his weddyng ryng
un to his wyf   of trewe affeccyoun,
praied hir come   to been at his deying,   520
66 And that she scholde   doon hir besy cure
by a maner   wyfly dyllygence
in haste ordeyne   for his sepulture
with no gret cost,   nor with no gret dyspence.   524
5 gan haste hir faste,   tyl she kam in presence,
where as he lay   dedly and pale of fface.
bespreynt with teris   knelyng with reverence
the dede body   swownyng she did enbrace.   528
67 And, as this notable   ffamous worthy knyght
sente hir to seyne   eek be his massangeer
in that place   to burye hym anoon right,
where as he lay,   afforn a smal auhteer,   532
5 and that she sholde   doon trewly hir deveer,
ffor hir silf   dyspoce and provyde
the XV. day   ffolwyng the same yeer
to be buryed   ffaste be his syde: 536
68 His hooly wyf   of al this thyng took heed,
lyk as Guy bad   (lyst no lenger tarye),
to quyte hir silf   of trouthe and womanheed:
she was ful loth   ffrom his desire to varye.   540
5 sente in al haste   ffor the ordynarye,
whiche ocupied   in that dyocyse:
she was nat ffounde   in o poynt contrarye
al thyng taccomplisshe,   as ye han herd devyse.   544
69 And this mater   breefly to conclude:
at his exequyes   old and yong of age
of dyverse statys   there cam gret multytude
with gret devocyoun   to that hermytage.   548
5 and lyk a prynce   with al the surplusage
they took hym up   and leyd hym in his grave

ordeyned of god
ageyn the Danys
70 Whos sowle, i hope,
with hooly spiritis
Ffelyce, his wyf,
the day approchyng
5 afforn ordeyned
hir sone Reynborne
heyr trewly born
in the erldam
71 The stok descendyng
to Guy, his ffader,
affter whos deth
Reynborne to entre
5 affter al this
hath yolde hir dette~
beside hir lord
with a good ende
72 For more auctorite
whos translacioun
out of the latyn
callyd of old
5 wich wrot the dedis
of them, that wern
gretly comendyng
Guy of Warwyk
73 Of whos noblesse
his marcyal name
the XI. chapitle
the parfight lyf,
5 his wylful povert,
brought on to me
yif ought be wrong
putteth the wyte
74 Meekly compiled
lyf of sir Guy
sette a syde
because he hadde
5 (in Tullius gardyn

afforn of hih corage
thys regyoun to save;   552
restith now in glorye
above the ffirmament.
ay callyng to memorie
of hir enterment   556
in hir testament
be tytle of hir possede
by lyneal dyscent
of Warwyk to succede   560
of antyquyte
be tytle of mariage,
of lawe and equyte
in to his herytage.   564
his mooder of good age
by deth un to nature:
in the hermytage
was maad hir sepulture.   568
as of this mateer,
is suych in sentence
maad by the cronycleer
Gerard Cornubyence,   572
with gret dilligence
in Westsex crowned kynges,
for knyghtly excellence
in his famous writynges,   576
ful gret heed he took
puttyng in remembraunce
of his historyal book — —
the vertuous governaunce,   580
hard goyng and penaunce
a chapitle to translate:
in metre or in substaunce
for dulnesse on Lydgate.   584
under correccyoun
by dyllygent labour,
pryde and presumpcioun,
of cadence no colour   588
he gadrid never fflour

nor of Omerus   he kam never in the meede),
praying echon   of support and ffavour
nat to dysdeyne   the clauses whan they reede.   592

    E x p l i c i t.

Anmerkungen.

1, 2 twen'ty and sévene: Die Betonung schwebt sehr
häufig zwischen dem einsilbigen Auftakte und der ersten Hebung; vgl. z. B. 1, 4 reg'nyng that týme. 2, 2 chir'chis, col-
légis. 2, 3 myh'ty castéllis. 55, 7 kept' among mén. 57, 1
‚Ser'tys‘ quod Guý. 73, 8 put'teth the wýte. 74, 1 meek'ly
compíled und un'der corrèccyoún u. s. w.

1, 8 thorugh oút ál this lánd ist wohl zu betonen, so dass
zweisilbiger Auftakt stattfände und zwischen der ersten und
zweiten Hebung die Senkung fehlte. Zweisilbiger Auftakt ist
häufig: z. B. 6, 6 oon of thés. 9, 8 thouh kyng Éthelstàn.
11, 3 cometh máy. 19, 1 this apoýntemént. 21, 6 callid ín.
55, 5 thorugh ál u. s. w. vgl. zu 2, 6. — Sichere Beispiele
von dem Fehlen der Senkung zwischen hochbetonten Hebungen
scheinen 25, 3 and bekám góddis knýght. 37, 7 to'ok his wéyę
ríght. 38, 1 í déem trewlý. 40, 6 képt hym si'lff clós. — Uebri-
gens ist gleich hier am Anfange des Gedichtes eine Anakoluthie
vorhanden: Lydgate gedachte wohl, als er die Strophe anfing,
fortzufahren: ‚geschah die Heldenthat Guy's‘; indessen die
Ausführung der letzten Zeitbestimmung ‚während der dänischen
Occupation‘ liess ihn die angefangene Construction aufgeben.
Es fehlen auf diese Weise sowohl Subject, wie Prädikat.
Dagegen 7, 1 fehlt nur das Prädikat, als das man etwa ‚wollte
nicht weichen‘ erwarten möchte: hier hat eine ursprünglich
wohl nur parenthetisch beabsichtigte Erklärung die Fortsetzung
des begonnenen Satzes verhindert. 72, 1 endlich fehlt wieder
Subject und Prädikat: hier ist die Veranlassung zur Anakoluthie
ein Relativsatz mit seinen Anhängseln.

2, 1 spared, nämlich they of Denmark. Häufig lässt Lydgate noch die Pronomina der 3. Person weg, wo der moderne

Sprachgebrauch sie verlangt: vgl. 4, 5. 20, 1. 25, 1. 26, 3. 7. 30, 1. 40, 6. 52, 7. 63, 5. 66, 5. 74, 1 u. s. w.

2, 3 every ist Hebung und Senkung, also die Hebung ist zweisilbig. Ebenso ist every gebraucht 21, 7. 30, 6. 40, 5. 41, 3. Vgl. hevenly 37, 2. 65, 5. bodyly 65, 4. many 8, 2 und fader 21, 7 ist Hebung. 72, 1 glaube ich, muss man lesen for móre ‚auctórite, so dass ori Hebung ist. Dagegen 70, 2 ist spirites zu betonen (vgl. ne. sprite, spright neben spirit) und natürlich auch dìsmerítees 9, 6; merítes 65, 5.

2, 6 they mad´en al wást and wýlde: so wie hier, kommt auch sonst zweisilbiger Auftakt in Verbindung mit schwebender Betonung vor. Vgl. 6, 4 the swerd´ of Bellóna. 13, 2 to schap´en in thís matéere. 18, 4 requyr´ed in háste. 20, 3 to tak´en hym tó prayéer. 20, 7 resem´bled in thér wepýng. 22, 4 and all´e þe provýncis. 24, 6 endew´ed with áll vertú. 56, 7 to tel´lyn his àventúre. 69, 7 ordeyn´ed of gód.

3, 8 distreyned. Das Verbum entspricht hier modernem constrain: ebenso Chaucer in Tr. u. Cr. 591: destreyne hire herte as faste to retourne, As thow doost myn to longen hire to see.

5, 1 for sum olde trespace gehört zum Vorhergehenden und zum Folgenden, steht also ἀπὸ κοινοῦ. Dieselbe Construction 22, 8 ffor his absence; 29, 1 for wach and trouble; 32, 7 a pilgrym; 48, 3 in inglyssh tonge; 58, 5 duryng my lyf; 66, 2 by a maner wyfly dyllygence; 70, 7 heyr trewly born; 74, 8 the clauses.

16, 4 with Colybrond . . . with hym: Wiederaufnahme eines Substantivs durch ein Pronomen auch 38, 5 Guy . . . he; 45, 5 my wil . . . it; 63, 3 Guy . . . he; vgl. 10, 2 Danys . . . ther.

16, 5 atween hem to : to natürlich Zahlwort.

16, 8 and háve poscéssioun, zwei Hebungen mit klingender Cäsur, obwohl z. B. 17, 2. 3. 5. 7 dylàcyoúne, conclùsioún, rèsignàcyoún, chàmpioún. Vgl. aber 18, 6 of thís convéncioun; 25, 2 of híh perféccyoun; 27, 7 but mèdyácioun u. s. w. Aehn- ich grácyous 31, 4; grácyouslỳ 29, 5; ffúrious 3, 1. 12, 7. 19, 2; ìnárcyal 12, 8. 18, 2. 73, 2; vértuous 73, 4 u. s. w.

17, 1 ff. ‚indem der König und die Herren, die dort zu-
gegen waren, sofort Antwort zu geben hatten': der Infinitiv
to yeve (V. 3) ist von dem zu ergänzenden being abhängig.
Vgl. 23, 2 born to ben his ffadris hayr hir yonge sone Raynborne to succede, indem ihr ihr junger Sohn R. nachfolgen sollte.
65, 3 god made hym knowe the day be an angel hys spirit
to conveye, durch einen Engel, welcher bringen sollte; vgl.
auch zu 71, 4. 58, 2.

20, 1 ff. accordýng, ffastýng, tarýng, wepýng: schwebende
Betonung im Reime; vgl. levýng, takýng 40, 4. 7; deyíng
65, 6; writýnges 72, 8; trewlý 38, 1; manhéede 23, 5; glad-
nésse 60, 2; Lydgáte 73, 8.

27, 5 from my synnes turne away thy cheere disespeired
stondyng in doubyll were, da ich verzweifelt dastehe in dop-
pelter Bekümmerniss (were s. Halliwell und Mätzners Sprachpr.
I, 1 S. 120, 239): stondyng ist absolutes Participium, dessen
Subject, wenn es ein persönliches Pronomen sein sollte, auch
sonst weggelassen wird; vgl. 48, 5 meetyng to gedre there
men myghte see terryble strokys, da sie zusammen kamen;
s. auch zu 58, 2.

54, 5 with al' the comoúnte: zweisilbiger Auftakt mit
schwebender Betonung (zu 2, 6), comoúnte mit zurückgetretenem
Accent (vgl. zu 16, 8. 72, 1).

58, 2 sool be our silff, indem wir allein für uns sind: es
ist sowohl das absolute Part. being (zu 17, 1) als dessen Subject we (zu 27, 5) zu ergänzen.

63, 1 habe ich myn geschrieben, da sonst my, thy nur
vor Consonanten (ausser h) gebraucht wird: vgl. z. B. 28, 1
my feith, myn hope, my trust, myn affyaunce.

67, 3 a'noon verlangt der Rhythmus: dies ist, wenn ich
nicht irre, das einzige Beispiel von schwebender Betonung im
inneren Vers.

70, 2 with hool'y spiri'tes lese ich mit zweisilbigem Auftakt und schwebender Betonung; vgl. zu 2, 6 u. 2, 3.

70, 7 construire ich ἀπὸ κοινοῦ (zu 5, 1): ausserdem ist
aus in the erldam V. 8 zu possede V. 6 the erldam zu denken.

71, 4 being ist zu ergänzen: s. zu 17, 1; whos im Sinne von his, wie lat. cuius = eius. Wegen dieses Gebrauchs des Relativs vgl. 29, 6. 8. 30, 7. 52, 1. 64, 5. 70, 1.

72 For móre auctórite: die zweite Hebung zweisilbig (zu 2, 3), der Accent zurückgetreten (54, 5. 16, 8). Als Subject und Prädikat, das der Dichter zu setzen vergessen hat, schwebte ihm, als er die Strophe anfing, etwa vor, ‚berufe ich mich auf Girardus Cornubiensis‘: vgl. 1, 8.